# SHAKING THINGS UP

## 14 YOUNG WOMEN WHO CHANGED THE WORLD

For my daughters, Emily and Allison,
and for my granddaughters, Sophie and Molly
—S.H.

Shaking Things Up: 14 Young Women Who Changed the World
Text copyright © 2018 by Susan Hood
Illustrations: pages 8–9 © 2018 by Shadra Strickland; pages 10–11
© 2018 by Hadley Hooper; pages 12–13 © 2018 by Lisa Brown;
pages 14–15 © 2018 by Emily Winfield Martin; pages 16–17 © 2018
by Sara Palacios; pages 18–19 © 2018 by Erin K. Robinson; pages
20–21 © 2018 by Sophie Blackall; pages 22–23 © 2018 by Melissa
Sweet; pages 24–25 © 2018 by Oge Mora; pages 26–27 © 2018 by
Isabel Roxas; pages 28–29 © 2018 by Julie Morstad; pages 30–31 ©
2018 by LeUyen Pham; pages 32–33 © 2018 by Selina Alko

Library of Congress Control Number: 2017949439
ISBN 978-0-06-269945-9 — ISBN 978-0-06-274172-1 (pbk.)

Design by Chelsea C. Donaldson
21 22 23 24 25  RTLO  10 9 8 7 6 5 4 3 2 1
❖
First Edition

# SHAKING THINGS UP

## 14 YOUNG WOMEN WHO CHANGED THE WORLD

By Susan Hood

Illustrated by Selina Alko • Sophie Blackall • Lisa Brown
Hadley Hooper • Emily Winfield Martin • Oge Mora
Julie Morstad • Sara Palacios • LeUyen Pham • Erin K. Robinson
Isabel Roxas • Shadra Strickland • Melissa Sweet

**HARPER**
*An Imprint of HarperCollinsPublishers*

# CONTENTS

Women and girls have been shaking things up for a long time, resisting those who would box them in. Here are fourteen inspiring young rebels (one just six years old, another only thirteen) who broke down walls to pursue their interests, talents, and rights. They fought fires, discovered prehistoric animals, circled the globe, braved Nazis, championed sports, changed the way we eat, integrated schools, improved medicine, and reached for the skies. The world is a better place for all of us because they dared to step out of the box. So don't ever let anyone tell you what you should or shouldn't do, can or cannot be. As journalist Nellie Bly said, "If you want to do it, you can do it!"

# TIMELINE

## EARLY 1780s

Firefighter **Molly Williams** is in her early thirties when she is named an official firefighter of the volunteer Oceanus Engine Company No. 11 in New York City, near the time of the American Revolution.

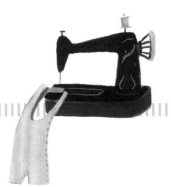

## 1907 OR '08

Swimming champion **Annette Kellerman** is in her early twenties when she is arrested at Revere Beach in Massachusetts for her "indecent" swimsuit. It was a forerunner of the modern one-piece bathing suit, which helped speed future swimming champ Gertrude Ederle across the English Channel in 1926.

## 1914

World War I begins in Europe.

## 1920

The 19th Amendment is passed, giving American women the right to vote.

## 1943

Secret agent **Jacqueline Nearne** parachutes into Nazi-occupied France to join the French Resistance as a courier at age 26.

## 1944

Secret agent **Eileen Nearne** joins the Resistance as a wireless operator in Paris at age 22. She is captured by the Gestapo but escapes in 1945.

## 1954

The United States Supreme Court declares public school segregation unconstitutional.

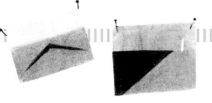

## 1981

Architecture student **Maya Lin**, at age 21, wins a competition to design the Vietnam Veterans Memorial, 8 years after the United States pulled out of the Vietnam War in 1973.

## 1992

Astronaut **Mae Jemison** becomes the first African American woman in space, blasting off in the space shuttle *Endeavour* at age 35.

## 1812

Fossil hunter **Mary Anning** is 13 years old when she unearths the first ichthyosaur skeleton known to London scientists.

## 1890

Investigative journalist **Nellie Bly** completes the fastest round-the-world trip of her day at age 25, traveling without an airplane. (The Wright Brothers' plane wasn't invented until 13 years later!)

## 1921

Author and librarian **Pura Belpré** is hired at age 22 by the New York Public Library, 10 years after it opened, to buy bilingual books and bring the city's growing Hispanic communities into the library.

## 1939

Artist Frida Kahlo sells a 1938 painting called *The Frame* to the Louvre museum in Paris at age 31. It's the first time the work of a 20th-century Mexican artist is purchased by a major museum.

## 1939

World War II begins when Germany invades Poland.

## 1960

Civil rights icon Ruby Bridges is just 6 years old when she becomes the first African American child to integrate an all-white school, in New Orleans, Louisiana.

## 1971

Anti-hunger activist **Frances Moore Lappé** publishes her book *Diet for a Small Planet* at age 27, selling more than 3 million copies and changing the way America eats.

## 1972

Title IX passes, stating that no person in the United States shall, on the basis of sex, be excluded from participation in any program receiving federal funds. It opens the door for women in sports, math, science, and more.

## 2011

High school student **Angela Zhang** wins $100,000 in the 2011–12 Siemens Competition in Math, Science & Technology for her cancer research at age 17.

## 2014

Girls' education activist **Malala Yousafzai** is awarded the Nobel Peace Prize at age 17, the youngest winner ever.

"As good a fire laddie as many of the boys
who . . . bragged at being such."

# TAKING THE HEAT

**Molly Williams, First Known Female Firefighter in the United States**

Years past in New York City streets
a blizzard whipped the air.
Despite the heavy falling snow,
a FIRE scorched the square!

The steeples clanged the town alarm!
Boy runners spread the news,
but firemen were sick abed
with influenza blues.

A local servant knew the drill;
she'd seen what must be done.
She hauled the pumper truck by hand,
adept as anyone.

In raging flames and choking smoke,
brave Molly took the heat.
With hose and axe, she met the blaze
to save the house and street.

The fire laddies gave her praise,
respect where it was due,
dubbed her Volunteer 11—
a member of the crew.

She glowed with pride, a pioneer!
She blazed a path, it's true,
yet women weren't hired here
'til 1982!

MARY (*nicknamed* MOLLY) DURHAM WILLIAMS (1747–1821) was an indentured servant of volunteer firefighter James Aymar. She knew the duties of the Oceanus Engine Company No. 11 from her time cooking for the men and didn't hesitate to help. There wasn't another female firefighter in New York City until 1982, when Brenda Berkman burned the FDNY with a discrimination lawsuit and won.

Art by Shadra Strickland

Plesiosaur

Ichthyosaur

"The greatest fossilist the world ever knew" —Hugh Torrens,
British Society for the History of Science

# BURIED TREASURE

### Mary Anning, Paleontologist

A
jaw,
mouth,
eyeholes,
a long skull.
What could it be?

Mary dug and drilled
uncovering "snakestones"

layers of limestone
and "crocodile teeth"

fossils sold to save her family from starving.
Patiently, persistently,
she chipped and chiseled the skull,
detecting a backbone—
blown bare in a storm.
Day after day she carved,
millions of years melting away,
revealing ribs, a spine,
etching the Earth's past
in the cliffs.
She worked,
unearthing

fabulous flippers

and a
long
tail:
an
i
c
h
t
h
y o s a u r !

like a dolphin's,

Penniless after her father's death, MARY ANNING (1799–1847) combed England's coast selling fossils to tourists. While her brother spotted a skull in 1811, it was thirteen-year-old Mary who unearthed the prehistoric sea reptile—an ichthyosaur—in 1812. Later, she discovered the first two complete plesiosaurs and a pterosaur, laying the foundation for Charles Darwin's theory of evolution.

# WOMAN OF THE WORLD

### Nellie Bly, Investigative Journalist

This ace reporter Nellie Bly
delivered headline news
by going undercover
in jails, ballets, and zoos.

A fearless writer of her day,
she righted wrongs along the way.

What's next? young Nellie wondered.
A trip like Jules Verne's book—
*Around the World in 80 Days?*
No, *faster*! That's her hook!

Her manager pooh-poohed her plan—
a trip like this would need a man!

So Nellie told him, "Start the man."
She'd beat him if she could.
The manager looked up and said,
"Yes, I believe you would!"

Bly hopped a ship and told her tale
of all she saw on Earth.
She wrote of camels, temples, jewels
with gutsy wit and mirth.

She rode on sampans, rickshaws, trains,
through blizzards, heat, and monsoon rains.

She talked with geishas, captains, priests;
she even met Jules Verne.
She brought a little monkey home
upon her proud return.

The worldwide press sang Nellie's praise.
She'd beaten Verne by eight whole days!

At twenty-five, young Nellie aced
a record-breaking race.
No soul on Earth had ever sped
the globe at such a pace!

**NELLIE BLY** (1864–1922) was the pen name of Elizabeth Jane Cochran, who impersonated a madwoman in an asylum, masqueraded as a ballerina, and posed as a thief—all to expose corruption and cruelty in hospitals, theaters, and prisons. She achieved worldwide fame for her race around the globe, clocking in at 72 days, 6 hours, 11 minutes, and 14 seconds. Later, in World War I, Nellie went to the front lines—becoming one of the first women war correspondents.

Art by Lisa Brown

"I want to swim. And I can't swim wearing more stuff
than you hang on a clothes line."

# TURNING THE TIDE

**Annette Kellerman, Champion Athlete and Inventor of the Modern Swimsuit**

There once was a mermaid queen,
lovely and lithesome and lean,
who swam afternoons
*without* pantaloons—
her swimsuit was deemed obscene!

The lady was quickly arrested.
Unafraid, she calmly protested:
Who can swim fifty laps
wearing corsets and caps?
Her statement could not be contested.

She streamlined the suit of the day
and invented our water ballet.
By changing the fashions
she fueled swimming passions
as women made waves in the spray.

Australian **ANNETTE KELLERMAN** (1886–1975) wore braces on her legs as a child, possibly due to rickets. Her doctor suggested swimming to strengthen her leg muscles. She went on to win world records, perform daredevil diving stunts, and star in silent films, popularizing a new one-piece bathing suit and ushering in a new age of athleticism for women.

Once in Puerto Rico
When We Were Very Young
Pérez y Martina
KIDNAPPED
A Little Princess
*The Story Girl*
They Loved to Laugh

*"I wished to be like Johnny Appleseed . . . to plant my story seeds across the land."*

# THE STORYTELLER

Pura Belpré, Children's Author and First Latina Librarian at the New York Public Library

**A**uthor, *amiga*

**B**ilingual-book buyer

**C**ommunity champion for children

**D**efender of the downtrodden

**E**mpowering educator

**F**olklorist, fairy-tale teller

**G**rower of gifts

**H**arlem history maker

**I**nner-city innovator

**J**oyful Johnny Appleseed

**K**nown for *Pérez y Martina*

**L**egendary Latina librarian

**M**ulticultural mosaic maker

**N**ew York narrator for *niños*

**O**utgoing organizer

**P**uerto Rican puppeteer

**Q**uerida

**R**ole model

**S**panish "story seed" sower

**T**rilingual translator

**U**plifter of the underprivileged

**V**oice of the voiceless

**W**eaver of wonder

e**X**pert in *español*

**Y**oung at heart

**Z**ealot

**PURA BELPRÉ** (1899–1982) revolutionized New York City by enticing Spanish-speaking communities inside the previously "English only" libraries. She bought Spanish books, conducted bilingual story hours, and celebrated Hispanic traditions. When she couldn't find Spanish tales on the shelves, she wrote them herself, publishing many children's books.

Art by Sara Palacios   **17**

"I am broken. But I am happy to be alive as long as I can paint."

# BROKEN

### Frida Kahlo, Artist

Broken from polio at age six,
from a withered foot,
childhood bullies shouting, *Frida pata de palo—*
*Frida peg leg.*

Broken again from a bus accident when she was eighteen—
   spine, collarbone,
            pelvis, ribs,
                  leg, and foot, smashed—
confined to bed in a full-body cast.
With an easel on her lap and a mirror above her bed,
Frida painted self-portraits.
"I am the subject I know best."
She breathed in the colors, handicrafts, carvings, clothing
of her homeland—Mexican, Aztec, Mayan.
Art flowed from her fingertips—
paintings of skulls, skeletons, stags, flowers, fantasy, fragility.

Surrealism is the stuff of dreams and nightmares,
but Frida said, "I paint my own reality"—
Mexico, misfortune, monkeys, misery, marriage to Diego Rivera,
politics, parrots, passion . . . pain.

"Frailty, thy name is woman," wrote Shakespeare,
an idea echoing through the ages,
yet Frida embodied strength *despite* her pain,
achieving fame and worldwide acclaim.

FRIDA KAHLO (1907–54), born Magdalena Carmen Frieda Kahlo y Calderón, originally wanted to become a doctor, but ill health led to painting. She grew to become a cultural icon and a world-famous artist—the first twentieth-century Mexican artist to sell a painting to the Louvre museum in Paris. Today, her paintings sell for more than fifteen million dollars each.

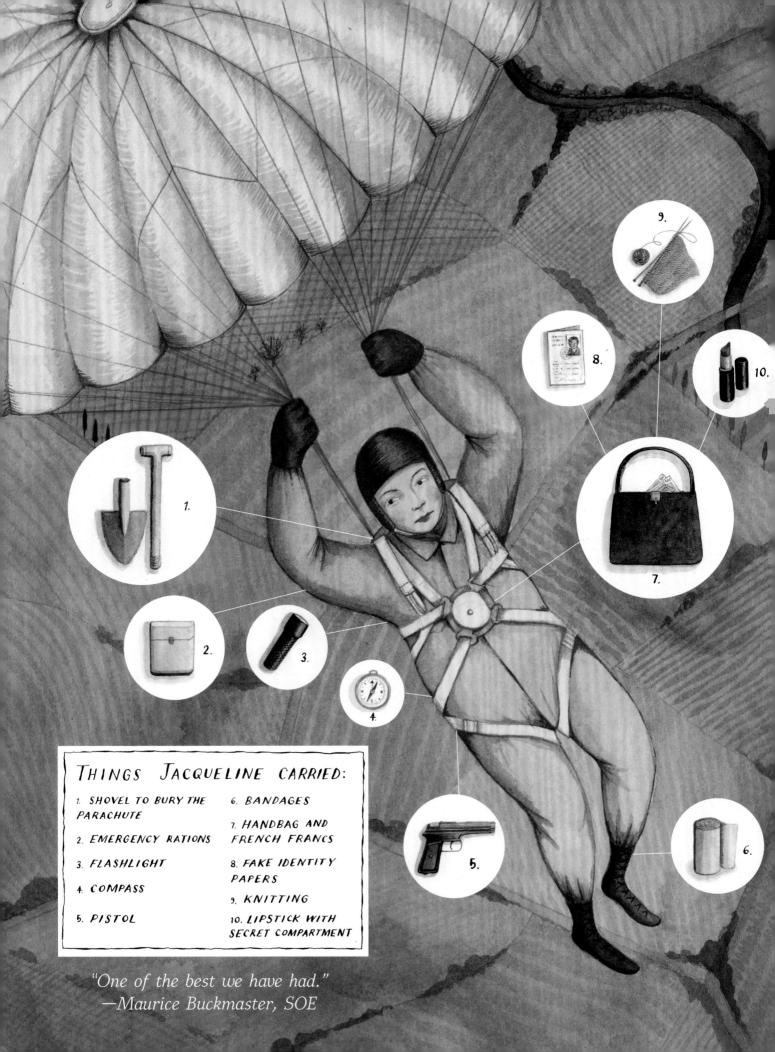

THINGS JACQUELINE CARRIED:

1. SHOVEL TO BURY THE PARACHUTE
2. EMERGENCY RATIONS
3. FLASHLIGHT
4. COMPASS
5. PISTOL
6. BANDAGES
7. HANDBAG AND FRENCH FRANCS
8. FAKE IDENTITY PAPERS
9. KNITTING
10. LIPSTICK WITH SECRET COMPARTMENT

"One of the best we have had."
—Maurice Buckmaster, SOE

# SECRET AGENT SISTERS

**Jacqueline Nearne, Undercover Operative**

down
    down
        down
jacqueline pulls the rip cord—
a blind drop
into nazi-occupied france of 1943,
code name—designer
her job—courier
of secret messages,
some in invisible ink
she's prepared to swallow them
if caught
all the enemy sees
is a lady with her knitting
hardly guessing there are
radio parts in her makeup bag,
she connects farmers, shopgirls, bakers,
all members of the resistance,
who stockpile supplies, weapons, cash
sabotage railways and factories
'til the americans arrive,
'til d-day is near!

**Eileen Nearne, Wireless Operator**

fourteen months later,
unbeknownst to jacqueline,
her younger sister, eileen (just 22),
flies into france
in the dark of night
into "a life in the shadows,"
code name—rose
her job—wireless operator
in paris's "wizard" network
tap-tap-tapping morse code to london
more than 100 messages sent,
but look out—
her transmitter is discovered
(jacqueline hears rumors
of eileen's arrest by the gestapo,
but nothing more. . . . is she alive?)


then
news of eileen's escape
from a prison camp—
the sisterhood survives!

*"It was a life in the shadows,
but . . . I was suited for it.
After the war, I missed it."*
*—Eileen Nearne*

Brave British sisters JACQUELINE NEARNE (1916–82) and EILEEN NEARNE (1921–2010) grew up in France and spoke flawless French—a sought-after talent for an SOE (Special Operations Executive) agent during World War II. Both were awarded France's prestigious Croix de Guerre medal and England's Member of the Order of the British Empire medal for their heroism.

Art by Sophie Blackall   

"Every choice we make can be a celebration of the world we want."

# FULL CIRCLE

**Frances Moore Lappé, Anti-Hunger Activist**

This is the Earth that Lappé dreamed,
the woman who wrote, "Eat more greens—"
broccoli, lettuce, squash, and beans—
who built a diet, a veggie cuisine,
that keeps our bodies strong and lean
that stops the wasteful Meat Machine
that feeds a local food routine
that saves the cost of gasoline
that keeps Earth's soil and water clean
that helps the hungry grow more beans,
cabbage, kale, and collard greens.
This is the Earth that Lappé dreamed.

**FRANCES MOORE LAPPÉ** (born 1944) was twenty-seven when she wrote, "Hunger is human made." She proved it takes 2,500 gallons of water and 16 pounds of grain to produce one pound of steak; so the world's grain is going to feed cattle, not people. Her book *Diet for a Small Planet* said if we "eat local," "mostly plants," we can be healthier, prevent world hunger, *and* help save the Earth.

Art by Melissa Sweet    **23**

"Kids know nothing about racism.
It's adults [who] pass it on to kids."

# A NEW SCHOOL

## Ruby Bridges, Civil Rights Pioneer

Ruby had a new school—William Frantz.
Mama wanted the very best.
But who were these men with badges?
Ruby wasn't sure.

Screaming masses flanked the school—
men and women holding signs.
Perhaps a parade? "For Mardi Gras?"
Ruby wasn't sure.

One marshal said, "Don't look back."
Was that a gun at his side?
Just what did "segregation" mean?
Ruby wasn't sure.

Why did the grown-ups point at her
and pull their kids from school?
Why were they all so upset?
Ruby wasn't sure.

Why did she and Mama sit all day
in the office by themselves?
Had she done something wrong?
Ruby wasn't sure.

Ruby was banned from the lunchroom,
banned from recess every day.
Why did her daddy call her "brave"?
Ruby wasn't sure.

She spent first grade with Mrs. Henry
in a classroom just for one.
Where were the other children?
Ruby wasn't sure.

But Ruby "never missed a day,"
with her teacher by her side.
Two heroines stood hand-in-hand,
their bond a bridge for sure.

**RUBY BRIDGES** (born 1954) was just six years old when, escorted by four US marshals, she marched into an all-white school in New Orleans and became an icon of the civil rights movement. Only one teacher agreed to take her as a student, so Ruby and Barbara Henry spent first grade together in a class of one—reading, spelling, singing songs, and doing jumping jacks. In the fight to end segregation, little Ruby led the way.

*"Never be limited by other people's limited imaginations."*

# LiFT-OFF

## Mae Jemison, First Female African American Astronaut

An African proverb says, "No one shows a child the sky."
No need.
Head back, it's there in her eyes;
glittering stars, swirling galaxies
fill her, thrill her,
even though her kindergarten teacher says,
"You want to be a scientist?
Don't you mean a nurse?"
Even though she's a "scaredy-cat."
Afraid of the dark, she looks up.
Afraid of heights, she looks down.
She skins her shins and muddies her dress
because she needs to KNOW.
*A Wrinkle in Time*
and *Star Trek*'s Uhura
say women can be scientists,
even rocket scientists.
Ignition.
All systems are go.
Three
Two
One

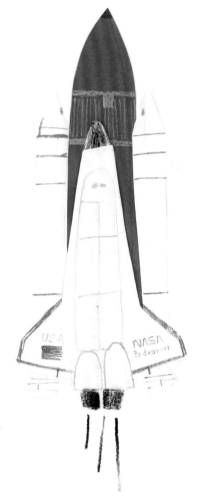

MAE JEMISON (born 1956) was "irritated that there were no women astronauts." She skipped seventh grade, started high school at age twelve, later earned a degree in medicine, and in 1987 was chosen for NASA's space program. When the space shuttle *Endeavour* launched in 1992, she was one of seven astronauts aboard.

*"To fly we have to have resistance."*

# A NEW VISION

### Maya Lin, Architect and Sculptor

In 1981, entry #1026 won
a competition
to build a memorial
to the fallen soldiers of Vietnam—
a controversial twenty-year war
where so many had died.

When Maya Lin's name was revealed,
some were outraged that
someone so young, just twenty-one,
someone Asian American,
someone female
had bested the best architects
to honor men killed in Vietnam
in a war we had not won.

Maya's design
was not perched high on a pedestal
but carved into the ground,
a long walk down
into the earth
and then back out again.

"I imagined taking a knife
and cutting into the earth," she said.
Like war, it would create a wound
that would heal with time but leave a scar.

Maya's design showed not a face or two
but more than 58,000 names—
spelling out, one by one,

just how many were lost;
it was not made
of traditional pure white marble
but black-as-night granite.

Maya Lin knew that,
polished to a high shine,
black granite is a mirror
for those who have come to reflect,
those present
who gaze into the past.

After all,
what should a war memorial do?
Unearth memory,
make us cry,
see ourselves,
and then lead us back up
into hope,
into the light.

MAYA LIN (born 1959) won the blind design competition unanimously despite the 1,441 entries that included the work of top architects. But when Lin's heritage, age, and gender were revealed, she had to appear before Congress to defend her vision. Today her memorial is visited by more than three million people each year.

"Failure is just an opportunity in disguise. You learn so much more from your 'failures' than anything else."

# BREAK IT DOWN

### Angela Zhang, Scientist and Cancer Researcher

Science,
my friend, I grew up with you.
When I was five,
you were a Harry Potter potion kit—
        I'd break flowers and leaves to mix
        in beakers with colored powders.
When I was seven,
you were my daddy's questions:
"Why is a manhole cover round?"
"Why do we see rainbows after it rains?"
"I don't know" wasn't an answer.
He taught me to break questions down,
        to chip away
        at the "black boxes of life."
When I was fourteen, I needed a lab
        and tools my high school didn't have.
I wrote to college professors,
whittling away at a wall of "No, no, no"
'til one at Stanford said, "Maybe,
        if you pass my test."

The catch? Homework—
scientific papers to read.
I highlighted the words I didn't know—
        all but the prepositions!
Then I remembered: Break it down.
I dissected the papers, word by word.
When I was fifteen, success!
I passed the test.
At Stanford, I chipped away
at the biggest black box of all—
        a cure for cancer.
Science, you are both stone and chisel,
and I, your willing apprentice,
        yearn to carve away life's mysteries
        as a sculptor chisels marble
        to find beauty inside.

ANGELA ZHANG (born 1994) invented a nanoparticle that can detect cancer cells and deliver medicine without harming healthy cells. At age seventeen, her work won her $100,000 in the 2011–12 Siemens Competition in Math, Science & Technology and a trip to the White House in 2012.

Art by LeUyen Pham    **31**

# BOOKS, NOT BULLETS

## Malala Yousafzai, Youngest Winner of the Nobel Peace Prize

She had been shot.
The bullet went in her left eye and out her left shoulder.

Flown to safety in England, Malala couldn't forget
the beatings, bodies, and bombs
back in her paradise valley of Pakistan. . . .
Her beloved school? Closed for girls.
Malala had spoken out.
Just eleven, she wrote a blog for the BBC.
"They are misusing the name of Islam," she said.
"Don't they know that the first word of the Holy Quran is *read*?"
Her mother feared for her life.
"The Taliban don't kill children," they said.
They were wrong.

The gunman stopped her school bus and asked for her by name.
He fired three bullets. One hit its mark.

The news ricocheted around the world,
but only her fear died that day.
She said, "Strength, power, and courage were born."

"I am those sixty-six million girls who are deprived of education."
Pens, not weapons, she preached. Books, not bullets.
The world heard and bestowed upon her its highest honor—the Nobel Peace Prize.

Malala.
One young girl who stood up.
One voice that would not be silenced.
She can change the world.

MALALA YOUSAFZAI (born 1997) shared the 2014 Nobel Peace Prize with Kailash Satyarthi from India. She will use the $500,000 prize to build secondary schools in Pakistan. In 2017, she launched the Gulmakai Network (named for Gul Makai, the pen name she used on her BBC blog). It pledges up to ten million dollars a year to support girls' education in developing countries such as Afghanistan, Lebanon, Nigeria, Pakistan, and Turkey.

Art by Selina Alko    **33**

# AUTHOR'S NOTE

"Never be limited by other people's limited imaginations," said astronaut Mae Jemison. Over the years, politics, religion, and "polite society" have tried to define what a woman should be, tried to restrict our behavior, speech, rights, aspirations, and even choice of clothing. But women have faced adversity head-on—defying poverty, illness, war, and discrimination—to change the world for men and women alike.

Choosing the fourteen movers and shakers in this book was the hardest part of the project (a good problem to have), and this is by no means an all-inclusive list. With young readers in mind, I decided to focus on girls and young women—a few well known, some little known, and a couple mostly unknown as yet. I chose a firefighter, an astronaut, a painter, and two secret agents, among others, who have stirred the pot and shaken up stereotypes, all to better the world.

Researching their stories, I was sometimes aghast at what they had to endure, but I was always in awe of their against-all-odds achievements. Take Mary Anning, who was eleven when her father died, leaving her family deeply in debt and close to starving. She earned money the only way she knew how, selling seaside fossils to British tourists. When she discovered an ichthyosaur at age thirteen and later unearthed plesiosaurs and a pterosaur, Mary helped split scientific theory wide open. Her groundbreaking finds helped pave the way for Charles Darwin's *On the Origin of Species*, published forty-seven years later, and a brand-new science—paleontology.

Activist Frances Moore Lappé said, "Every choice we make can be a celebration of the world we want." That's why I chose to write this book—to celebrate the world I want for my daughters, my granddaughters, and all the young girls and boys out there. I could never have guessed how much joy I would discover along the way.

—Susan Hood

# SOURCES, BOOKS, WEBSITES, AND MORE

**MARY ANNING** dug up evidence of evolution, shaking up the commonly accepted story of creation from the Bible.

**Note:** Sources debate the dates of the ichthyosaur find. Mary's brother found the skull in 1811, according to his son, but Mary found the entire skeleton in 1812. The *Western Flying Post* (a newspaper of the time) reported that the final excavation occurred in November 1812. Mary, born in May 1799, would have been thirteen years old.

The 1908 tongue twister "She sells seashells by the seashore," by Terry Sullivan, was inspired by Anning.

**Sources:** Quote p. 10: Hugh Torrens, "Presidential Address: Mary Anning (1799–1847) of Lyme; 'The Greatest Fossilist the World Ever Knew'," *The British Journal for the History of Science*, www.jstor.org/stable/4027645

*The Fossil Hunter: Dinosaurs, Evolution, and the Woman Whose Discoveries Changed the World* by Shelley Emling (Palgrave Macmillan, 2009)

**Further Resources:** BBC kids' site: www.bbc.co.uk/schools/primaryhistory/famouspeople/mary_anning

**NELLIE BLY** upended the nineteenth-century notion that a woman's place was in the home and helped blaze a path for a new style of newspaper reporting—investigative journalism.

**Sources:** Quotes pp. 12–13: All from *Around the World in Seventy-Two Days and Other Writings* by Nellie Bly (Penguin, 2014)

*Eighty Days: Nellie Bly and Elizabeth Bisland's History-Making Race Around the World* by Matthew Goodman (Ballantine, 2013)

*Bylines: A Photobiography of Nellie Bly* by Sue Macy (National Geographic, 2009); ages 10 and up

**Further Resources:** *The Daring Nellie Bly: America's Star Reporter* by Bonnie Christensen (Knopf, 2003); ages 5–8

I consulted a variety of sources to write this book, including interviews, books, websites, lectures, newspapers, videos, and conversations with museum and library experts. You can find many of the women in the book profiled here:

* Biography: biography.com

* *Encyclopedia Britannica*: Britannica.com

* MAKERS, the largest video collection of women's stories: makers.com

* National Women's Hall of Fame: womenofthehall.org

* National Women's History Museum: nwhm.org

For further resources, read on. For even more information and notes about the kinds of poetry used in the book, visit www.harpercollins.com/shakingthingsup.

## MOLLY WILLIAMS kindled the idea that women were brave enough to fight fires.

**Note:** There are many errors about Molly online, including a bogus photograph; photography had not yet been invented. Some mention the Blizzard of 1818, but Molly would have been seventy-one by then; the actual date is in the early 1780s. She worked for James Aymar, not Benjamin, who was born in 1791 (no relation). New York City Fire Museum records show Molly arrived in the city as an indentured servant, where she married a slave. Many assume that would affect her status, but Dr. Leslie Harris, coeditor of *Slavery in New York*, says there was no New York law enslaving spouses through marriage in the 1780s.

**Sources:** Quote p. 8: *Dennis Smith's History of Firefighting in America* (Doubleday, 1980)

*www.nycfiremuseum.org*

**Further Resources:** *Molly, by Golly! The Legend of Molly Williams, America's First Female Firefighter* by Dianne Ochiltree, illustrated by Kathleen Kemly (Calkins Creek, 2012); ages 6 and up

## ANNETTE KELLERMAN championed athleticism for women's health and self-confidence and popularized a new kind of swimsuit, freeing women from the confines of corsets and pantaloons.

**Note:** Sources disagree about Annette's birth date and the date of her arrest. According to author Shana Corey, her birth certificate says July 6, 1886, and many other primary sources place her at Revere Beach in July 1908.

**Source:** Quote p. 14: http://americanhistory.si.edu/object-project/ready-wear/bathing-suit

**Further Resources:** *Mermaid Queen* by Shana Corey, illustrated by Edwin Fotheringham (Scholastic, 2009); ages 4–8

News article about Annette's arrest with photos showing the evolution of bathing suits from 1830 to 1928, "This Woman's One-Piece Bathing Suit Got Her Arrested in 1907" by Kristin Toussaint, Boston.com, July 2, 2015

## PURA BELPRÉ translated "English-only" libraries into multicultural centers that reflected the growing Spanish-speaking population in New York City. Her work validated the Hispanic experience and opened windows to the world for all.

**Note:** There is some discrepancy about Belpré's birth date. It's been reported as February 2, 1899, December 2, 1901, and February 2, 1903; the earliest date is the most accepted.

**Sources:** Quote p. 16: *The Stories I Read to the Children: The Life and Writing of Pura Belpré, the Legendary Storyteller, Children's Author, and New York Public Librarian*, edited by Lisa Sánchez González (Centro Press, 2013)

Guide to the Pura Belpré Papers, https://centropr.hunter.cuny.edu/sites/default/files/faids/Belpre_Pura.pdf

**Further Resources:** *The Storyteller's Candle/La velita de los cuentos* by Lucía González, illustrated by Lulu Delacre (Lee & Low, 2008); ages 5–8

**FRIDA KAHLO** illustrated that disability doesn't have to destroy dreams.

**Sources:** Quotes pp. 18–19: All Kahlo quotes from "Mexican Autobiography," *Time* magazine (April 27, 1953)

"*Frailty, thy name is woman*" from *Hamlet* by William Shakespeare

*Frida: A Biography of Frida Kahlo* by Hayden Herrera (Harper, 1983)

**Further Resources:** *Frida* by Jonah Winter, illustrated by Ana Juan (Arthur A. Levine, 2002); ages 5–8

*Viva Frida* by Yuyi Morales, photography by Tim O'Meara (Roaring Brook, 2014); ages 4–8

Wonderful photos of Frida at the Smithsonian's Archives of American Art exhibit, www.aaa.si.edu/exhibitions/frida-kahlo

**JACQUELINE AND EILEEN NEARNE** are testaments to the courage of young women who resisted the horrors of Nazism in World War II.

**Source:** Quotes pp. 20–21: *A Cool and Lonely Courage: The Untold Story of Sister Spies in Occupied France* by Susan Ottaway (Little, Brown, 2013)

**Further Resources:** 1947 British docudrama film all about SOE agents set in France after the Liberation, starring Jacqueline Nearne herself! *School for Danger*

"Eileen Nearne, Wartime Spy, Dies at 89" obituary by John F. Burns, *New York Times*, www.nytimes.com/2010/09/22/world/europe/22nearne.html

**MAE JEMISON** launched African American women into space and now advocates for minorities in math and science.

**Sources:** Quote p. 26: "Mae Jemison: The First African American Woman in Space and First Real Astronaut on *Star Trek*" by Jolene Creighton, December 21, 2015

Quotes p. 27: *Find Where the Wind Goes: Moments from My Life* by Mae Jemison (Scholastic, 2001); ages 12 and up

**Further Resources:** *Mae Among the Stars* by Roda Ahmed, illustrated by Stasia Burrington (HarperCollins, 2018); ages 4–8

Facts about *Endeavour* and Mae's flight: www.nasa.gov/mission_pages/shuttle/shuttlemissions/archives/sts-47.html

Mae Jemison's website, www.drmae.com

**MAYA LIN** broke new ground with her modern vision in architecture.

**Sources:** Quote p. 28: *And I Quote: The Definitive Collection of Quotes, Sayings, and Jokes for the Contemporary Speechmaker*, revised edition, by Ashton Applewhite, William R. Evans III, and Andrew Frothingham (Thomas Dunne, 2003)

Quote p. 29: "Making the Memorial" by Maya Lin, *New York Review of Books*, November 2, 2000, www.nybooks.com/articles/2000/11/02/making-the-memorial

**Further Resources:** *Maya Lin: Artist-Architect of Light and Lines* by Jeanne Walker Harvey, illustrated by Dow Phumiruk (Henry Holt, 2017); ages 4–8

Video tour of the memorial, "Maya Lin, Vietnam Veterans Memorial," www.youtube.com/watch?v=wuxjTxxQUTs&t=79s

See more about the memorial and Maya's other work from the National Endowment for the Arts, "Maya Lin," www.youtube.com/watch?v=BsrLVPu5otI

**FRANCES MOORE LAPPÉ** stirred the pot, changing forever the way Americans eat in an effort to solve world hunger and preserve the planet.

**Sources:** Quote p. 22: Interview with Frances Moore Lappé

*Diet for a Small Planet,* 20th anniversary edition, by Frances Moore Lappé (Ballantine, 2011)

**Further Resources:** Frances Moore Lappé biography, Small Planet Institute, www.smallplanet.org/frances -moore-lappe

"Why Are We Creating a World That No One Wants?" Frances Moore Lappé's TED Talk, www.youtube.com/watch?v=w_Lw5lt3J6c

**RUBY BRIDGES** schooled Jim Crow America by making the Supreme Court's landmark decision to end segregation a reality.

**Sources:** Quote p. 24: "Ruby Bridges Shares the Key to Overcoming Racism," www.youtube.com/ watch?v=SvW10_kvKDA

Quotes p. 25: *Through My Eyes* by Ruby Bridges (Scholastic, 1999); ages 8–12; "Ruby Bridges Story," www.youtube.com/watch?v=JIg3jP1r-zM

**Further Resources:** *Ruby Bridges Goes to School: My True Story* by Ruby Bridges (Scholastic, 2009); ages 4–8

"Ruby Bridges: A Simple Act of Courage," http:// teacher.scholastic.com/activities/ruby-bridges/ruby-bridges-for-kids.htm

"Civil Rights Pioneer on First-Grade Teacher: 'She Showed Me Her Heart'," www.youtube.com/ watch?v=qwb5xsRO1yc

**ANGELA ZHANG** gave American medicine a shot in the arm, creating a possible cure for cancer.

**Sources:** Quotes pp. 30–31: All quotes from interview with Angela Zhang

**Further Resources:** "Breaking Down the Unknown," Angela Zhang at TEDxTeen, www.youtube.com/ watch?v=_pBLPrWle7g

"Teen Creates Cancer-Fighting Technique," *CBS Evening News with Scott Pelly,* www.youtube.com/ watch?v=c9NvBcyN7qE&feature=player_embedded

**MALALA YOUSAFZAI** risked death to teach the world to invest in education for girls.

**Note:** In 2017, the Malala Fund estimated that more than thirty-two million girls do not attend primary school and ninety-eight million are missing out on a secondary education.

**Sources:** Quote p. 32: *He Named Me Malala,* directed by Davis Guggenheim, 2015

Quotes p. 33: "Malala: We Must Talk to the Taliban to Get Peace," BBC News, October 7, 2013, www.bbc. com/news/world-24333273; Malala Yousafzai—Nobel Lecture, www.nobelprize.org/nobel_prizes/peace/ laureates/2014/yousafzai-lecture_en.html; "Malala at Youth Takeover Event," July 12, 2013, www.un.org/press/en/2013/dev3009.doc.htm

**Further Resources:** Read Malala's diary for the BBC, "Moving Moments from Malala's BBC Diary," October 10, 2014, www.bbc.com/news/world-asia-29565738

*Malala's Magic Pencil* by Malala Yousafzai, illustrated by Kerascoët (Little, Brown, 2017); ages 4–8

# ACKNOWLEDGMENTS

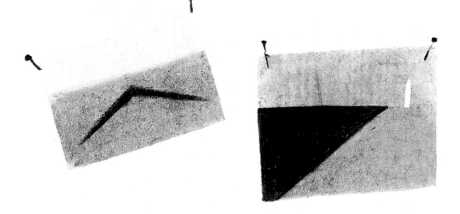

Thanks to the following invaluable experts: Dan Abernethy, VP, Sotheby's; Richard Bull, volunteer curatorial and research assistant, Lyme Regis Museum; Shana Corey, author of *Mermaid Queen*; Dr. John Maisey, curator-in-charge, Division of Paleontology, American Museum of Natural History; Marysol Nieves, VP, specialist, Latin American Art, Christie's; Lisa Sánchez González, professor, University of Connecticut; and the staff of the New York City Fire Museum. Thanks also to Liisa Hibbard (MLS); Karen Jordan, fellow author; and Christopher Kueffner, grades 4–5 teacher.

I'm especially grateful to Paul, a supportive husband and father, who always has my back. I couldn't have written this book without you.

Shout-outs and special thanks to the wonder women behind this book—Nancy Inteli, Chelsea C. Donaldson, Cheryl Eissing, Honee Jang, Bethany Reis, Jill Davis, Allison Brown, Brenda Bowen, and all the spectacular illustrators. I loved making this book with you!